LifeCaps Presents:

Sí Se Puede

A Biography of Cesar Chavez

By Paul Brody

BookCaps™ Study Guides

www.bookcaps.com

PAUL BRODY

Copyright © 2013 by Golgotha Press, Inc.

Cover Image © branchecarica - Fotolia.com.

All rights reserved. This book or any portion thereof may not be reproduced or used in any manner whatsoever without the express written permission of the publisher except for the use of brief quotations in a book review.

Printed in the United States of America

Sí Se Puede

Table of Contents

About LifeCaps 6
Introduction 7
Chapter 1: Growing Up in Yuma 10
    Family History 10

    Birth and Early Childhood 11

    School and Church 12

    The Great Depression 13

    An End to Childhood 15

Chapter 2: Farm Work 18
    Surviving in California 18

    School and Segregation 21

    Teenage Rebellion and the Navy 22

    Building a Family 23

Chapter 3: Getting Involved in Activism 26
    Fred Ross and CSO 26

    Becoming an Organizer 29

    Resigning from CSO 31

Chapter 4: Forming the Union 32
    Gathering Strength.. 32

    The Grape Strike 35

    Three Hundred Miles to the First Contract......... 37

    Merger 38

    Influential Fast 41

Chapter 5: Expanding the UFWOC..................... 45
    Political Tragedy and New Threats....................... 45

    Conquering Delano 47

    Teamster Violence 49

    Boycott, Jail Time, and Assassination Contracts 51

    Leaving California 53

    Fighting the Teamsters 55

    Farm Workers Bill of Rights 57

    Animal Rights Activism 58

    Family and Personal Life 59

Chapter 6: Controversies 62
    Anti-Immigration Stance.. 62

    Disorganization and Paranoia................................ 63

Chapter 7: Death and Legacy 67

Sí Se Puede

Cesar Chavez Bibliography 69
    Internet Sources 69

    Print Sources 70

    Documentaries 70

PAUL BRODY

ABOUT LIFECAPS

LifeCaps is an imprint of BookCaps™ Study Guides. With each book, a lesser known or sometimes forgotten life is recapped. We publish a wide array of topics (from baseball and music to literature and philosophy), so check our growing catalogue regularly (www.bookcaps.com) to see our newest books.

Sí Se Puede

INTRODUCTION

Cesario Estrada Chavez, more commonly known as Cesar Chavez, was a highly influential activist worker who created a union for farm workers all across the United States. A California farm worker himself, Cesar understood first-hand the injustice that laborers experienced - the low wages, long hours, horrible living conditions, and constant exposure to pesticides. He was manipulated by labor contractors and his family traveled from farm to farm every season looking for work, trapped in the cycle of poverty by the world of agriculture.

Eventually, after his farming days were behind him, Cesar got involved in community organizing and became passionate about not just escaping from the growers, but changing the entire system to provide fair wages and living conditions for farm workers in California, and eventually all across the United States. He continued on, going from being a standard community organizer to breaking free and forming his own union that would keep the specific needs of the farm workers in mind.

The union grew, and as its presence began to influence the market the battles between the union, the growers and the government intensified. The union used every nonviolent strategy in their book, including strikes, boycotts, lawsuits, marches, and rallies to bring support to their cause. The fledgling union faced not only the growers, but the entire business of agriculture which was backed by the government and, therefore, powerful. Their hopes lie in the people - the farm workers and consumers all across the United States. The growers fought back with threats of violence, throwing strikes in jail, and eventually forming their own union as a shield against Cesar Chavez and his followers. After many years, however, Cesar's leadership, determination, and focus on non-violence prevailed.

A man of many facets, Cesar was intelligent, hardworking, and stubborn enough to not only become the leader of the organization but to keep it going throughout the years. His quiet passion, willingness to help others, and strong religious beliefs all worked together to bring the farm workers, and organizers together to make the union and turn its goals into reality. He famously organized marches, underwent lengthy fasts and lived a life of poverty for the sake of his cause.

Many organizations and activists before him had attempted to unionize the farm workers in California, but Cesar Chavez was the first to succeed. For his efforts and accomplishments, he is celebrated as a great advocate for equality and non-violence, especially among the Latin American population, where his name is often mentioned in reverence, and his famous motto "Si Se Puede" (which roughly translates to "it is possible") is still used to inspire hope. Cesar Chavez's legacy remains in the form of monuments, buildings, and streets dedicated to the activist hero, as well as a national holiday on March 31, his birthday. In modern day, his non-violent efforts and goals are often compared to other famous peaceful activists such as Gandhi.

CHAPTER 1: GROWING UP IN YUMA

Family History

Cesar's rich Mexican heritage undoubtedly influenced his momentous work in activism, and led to him becoming a symbol for the Latin American population. It was in the 1880's that his grandfather, whom Cesar later called Papa Chayo, escaped the Hacienda del Carmen, where he was treated like a slave. Rebelling against the growers in Mexico, he crossed the border into Texas and earned enough money from his railroad job to bring his wife and fourteen children into America in 1888.

The large family settled in the Yuma Valley in Arizona, next to the Colorado River. Cesar's father, a strong, six foot tall man, worked the fields and helped build a homestead and farm on the land. Originally, the land in Yuma was dry and desertlike, but the building of the dam allowed it to be transformed into a farmer's paradise. Cesar's father stayed on the farm, and in his thirties married Cesar's mother, a tiny, talkative woman named Juana Estrada.

In 1925, Cesar's father bought several stores and opened up businesses. He ran everything from a small grocery store to a pool hall. Since the large family never truly moved away (most settled close to the farm) business was profitable enough to start a family of his own.

Birth and Early Childhood

Cesario (later shortened to Cesar) Chavez was born in the back of his father's store on March 31, 1927. He was named Cesario after his grandfather. Two years later, Cesar's brother Richard was also born, and because of their small age difference the two were remarkably close growing up.

Cesar spent his early childhood surrounded by a close and loving family. His father was a stern man, but also acutely patient. He showed his affection for the family by working hard and taking care of them. Every day he worked in the fields, while his mother took care of the house. The more lenient parent, Cesar's mother was openly loving towards all of her children and had a strong sense of good which she strived to pass on to them. She told her children stories and proverbs, and taught her them to solve their problems without violence. She was a generous soul, always willing to give help to those in need.

School and Church

While Cesar's oldest sister Rita was adept at school and enjoyed going, the educational environment bored Cesar. The school that the children attended was remarkably small, consisting of only three rooms. In the minority as Mexican-Americans, Cesar and his siblings were punished for speaking Spanish and were required to learn English. The semi-racist environment caused an identity crisis in the young Cesar Chavez, who did not know how to define himself as a Mexican, American, and citizen. Perhaps in a different school, without the looming presence of discrimination and embarrassment, Cesar would have enjoyed the learning experience.

Instead, he found his solace in religion. Although he did not attend church until he was a little older, his mother made sure that they all had a thorough Catholic education. Cesar and his siblings were trained by their grandmother, Mama Tella, who was in charge of group prayers and evening gatherings in the family. The Christian religion in particular played a massive role in Cesar's future activism work, but he was taught to respect all faith.

The Great Depression

Cesar's father, already owning several successful small businesses, tried to expand by becoming a landowner. He made a deal with a neighbor to clear off eighty acres of land in exchange for keeping forty. When his father finished the work, he found out that the neighbor had already sold the land to another farmer. A lawyer advised Cesar's father to take out a loan and buy the land back, which he did.

Not soon after this betrayal, however, the Great Depression hit and the family's situation took a turn for the worse. During the depression, Cesar's father tried to feed the extended family out of the small grocery store he ran, but eventually went bankrupt and was forced to move back into the original farmhouse built by Papa Chayo. Unable to pay back the debt on the additional farmland, he was forced to sell the land at a loss, and was betrayed again when the lawyer who advised him to take out a loan in the first place ended up buying the acreage for himself.

By 1932, having lost the land and the businesses, the family of six was sharing a single room in Papa Chayo's homestead. Cesar and Richard slept on an old pool table from the abandoned pool hall, and all the children helped work on their grandfather's farm. Although the family did not have money and were forced to barter for the things they needed, things were not all bad. There was still enough food being produced by the farm to feed the family, and Cesar's mother sold eggs and milk at the market.

In 1933, the family farm experienced the first of several yearly droughts. In addition to the economic hardships, tensions were also becoming worse in the valley due to violence between the whites and the Mexican Americans. Cesar's first cousin was drowned by a white grower, who was suspected of murdering him in order to claim his life insurance. The grower was later convicted of larceny, and the incident heated up racial tensions on both sides. 1936 saw a new influx of workers for the dam, and Cesar experienced even more discrimination in school than before due to the increased number of whites.

While school was unpleasant and confusing, Cesar enjoyed a relatively good life at home. With such a large extended family, there was always good company and warmth to be found. Surrounded by his culture and family, Cesar enjoyed working on the

Sí Se Puede

farm, night-time BBQs, and listening to stories from the older generation about the Mexican Revolution and escaping from the haciendas in the old country. He became talented at playing pool at his father's hall, and took odd jobs to help the family survive.

But in 1937, despite the families' best efforts, they were deep in debt. Cesar's father, who was becoming older, owed over four thousand dollar in land taxes to the government. Unable to pay, the farmland was seized by the government that summer.

An End to Childhood

Even though they had lost the farm, Cesar's father did not give up hope. Believing that he could buy the precious farmland back, he set out for California in the summer of 1938 looking for farm work. After he had found a job, he sent for the rest of the family, who piled in an old car for the road trip. Cesar remembered being stopped in the middle of the night during that trip by the border patrol, who aggressively questioned the family for five hours. Cesar's mother, who was unable to speak English, worried that the family would be deported. Eventually, however, they were able to continue; the border patrol let them go and they made it to California without any further incident.

For the first time, Cesar and his siblings realized that they had been fortunate when they lived on the farm. Even though they were poor, they had always had food, shelter, kind neighbors and clean water. In their new, small, run down home, their belongings were stolen, the children were beat up, and the wages were so low the family was trapped in utter poverty. Realizing that they had to get out, Cesar's father bought a car with the last of the money that they had, and they traveled back to California for one more effort to win back the family farm.

In 1939, two years after the Chavez land had been taken by the government, the land went up for auction to the general public. Cesar's father entered the bidding and won. He had thirty days to get the money, or he would lose the land for good. With no income and no savings, he was forced to ask everyone he knew for loans. In the end, he was unable to borrow enough money to buy the farm, and so it went to the next highest bidder. Cesar and his family watched in despair as the land was sold and cleared out by tractors. Cesar was horrified at the destruction and disrespect for nature that the tractors wrought on the land as they tore up the land and trees he had grown up farming and playing on. Having lost their land for good, the family packed up all their belongings in the car and left Yuma, beginning a long and dangerous journey to Cali-

Sí Se Puede

fornia and into the world of unfair farm owners and manipulative labor contractors.

CHAPTER 2: FARM WORK

Surviving in California

Like many other impoverished families uprooted during the Great Depression, the Chavez family drove to California in the hopes of finding decent work on the huge farms across the coastal state. And, like many families before them, instead they found terrible conditions and growers who were all too willing to take advantage of the influx of desperate and starving poor.

In the beginning, Cesar and his family were easy prey for manipulative labor contractors. The contractors, who got paid per family, would target large families obviously homeless and out of work. They would get a tidy sum for themselves from the growers for the hiring, and in many cases the majority of the wages earned by the family on the farms. Large cars and vans full of belongings and children were a common sight in California during the Depression, and the Chavez family might as well have had a neon sign painted over their heads.

Out of money, and not knowing any better, the family followed a labor contractor to their first job - picking peas. The wages were horrible, and there was no housing to be found. Despite the conditions, they had no choice but to pick the peas and hope that they could make enough money to fill up their car and continue on. Soon, the work on that harvest was gone, and they moved on to a town called San Jose to pick cherries. Not long after that, it was apricots, then orchard apples.

In the winter, they picked walnuts, which was fearfully dangerous work. Cesar and Richard opened up a small business on the side of the road shelling walnuts for pennies. They would spend their free time on odd jobs, chopping wood and running errands. Everyone pooled their money, but, unable to afford any sort of housing, they slept outside in a tent. Even the tent was too small to fit the entire family, and Cesar and Richard slept outside. Eventually, they were given a shack by one of the more fortunate locals and spent the rest of the winter there.

After that first harsh winter, the family began following the crops every season along with thousands of other poor minorities. Cesar viewed firsthand the vicious cycle of workers who became labor contractors just to survive, and then used dirty tricks to steal time and money from the other workers. He saw labor camps, contractors taking advantage of young girls, and contractors who promised pay but never delivered.

Through it all, the family stayed together. Cesar's father never pushed the children to work, no matter how much they needed the money. Because of this, his children were willing to work even harder. Cesar's mother always helped those that she saw in need, even if it meant that the family might go without. They dug up beets, thinned lettuce and picked onions. They got burns and rashes on their hands and body from pesticides and hurt their backs from constant stooping.

After a few years, they had developed a pattern. In the winters, they would travel to Brawley to work on onions, broccoli, and lettuce. The summer provided a bounty of fruit and vegetables so the family had constant work traveling to keep up with harvests of melons, strawberries, and grapes, and numerous other fruits. The fall was cotton season. They traveled to the same places over and over, never breaking out of poverty, stuck in the loop of survival.

Sí Se Puede

School and Segregation

Despite the constant moving around and lack of funds, Cesar's mother always made sure that her children went to school. She believed that education was the only way for them to escape from the cycle of poverty that the family had found themselves in. Cesar and his siblings went to school, even though they had no shoes or good clothes to wear and experienced intense racism at many schools.

It became a ritual, on the first day in a new town, to seek out the school and enroll the children. Even if they only attended for a few days because they were busy working in the fields, they were still enrolled in school. By the time Cesar was done with his middle school education, he had attended thirty seven different schools. Oddly enough, his favorite schools were the ones where they segregated the whites and the minorities. While a more alarming practice on the whole, the segregation allowed Cesar to attend school without being bullied for his accent or low social status.

The racism did not end in the school system, however, and the Chavez family was often prevented from entering stores or establishments with "Whites Only" signs out front. As a child, this sort of treatment was simply part of life. It was only later that Cesar Chavez thought to question it.

When Cesar graduated middle school, he promised his aging mother that she would no longer have to work in the fields. He would work full time while she stayed home and tended the kitchen and clothing. His father was growing older as well, and so Cesar took over the schedule of crops, telling the family when it was time to move on to a new location. Even though it was just within the confines of his family, Cesar demonstrated a natural ability to take charge and lead.

Teenage Rebellion and the Navy

Like many teens, Cesar Chavez entered a stage of rebellion while he and his family were still working the farms all over California. He adopted a popular style of dress among the younger generation of Mexican Americans called Pachuco, modeled after the style of Mexican gangsters. He grew his hair out long and wore baggy clothes and, in the eyes of the older generation, generally looked disreputable. His dress made people nervous, and many times they were surprised to find him a polite and gentle young man. Cesar learned a valuable lesson about not judging people by their looks.

The Pachuco stage of Cesar's life did not last long, however, as he decided to join the Navy in 1944 in order to avoid the draft. He joined willingly so that he could pick the Navy instead of being put in the Army, and ended up a deck hand on a ship along with many other Mexican Americans. He hated the regimentation of the Navy, and his years there were some of the least favorite times.

It was significant, however, in that the regimentation combined with the constant racism and segregation, caused Cesar Chavez to challenge authority for the first time. While a small instance, sitting peacefully on the "white's only" side of the movie theatre, Cesar was threatened with jail for his crime. When he did not respond defensively or violently, he was left alone. In his own way, Cesar had discovered the power of non-violence in challenging authority.

Building a Family

After serving in the navy, Cesar got out and was reunited with his family. While they were making the rounds in Delano, California, Cesar met his future wife, Helen. She worked at the grocery store, and Cesar was a frequent customer. Cesar married Helen in 1948, when he was 28 years old.

Although Helen had lived in Delano her entire life, and had her mother and siblings to support financially, she decided to leave and travel around California with Cesar. He had a little money saved up, and they worked hard to keep afloat, just as his family had done since they moved to California. After a year and a half, their first son, Fernando, was born. They spent several years without any money, living on the fringes, but with a third child on the way Cesar landed a job at a lumber mill. It was a steady job, and the managers loved him because he was such a hard worker, and highly trustworthy. With a loving wife, a growing family, and a steady job, Cesar had managed to escape the cycle of the California farms.

With his new found free time, he began getting more involved in religion, and learned about Catholicism from Father McDonnel, a Catholic priest who Cesar greatly admired. He put his education to good use and started reading and learning. He read about Saint Francis, the man who gave up worldly possessions and lived a life of poverty, and Gandhi, the great advocate of non-violence.

Of all the leaders Cesar read about, he admired Gandhi the most because he put his duty first above all else. Not only that, but Cesar admired the way that Gandhi set the example for non-violent behavior, and put the only thing he had, his body, on the line for his cause. While Cesar had grown up influenced by his mother's non-violent beliefs, and even used non-violence to his advantage, he had never realized how powerful non-violence could actually be, how it could change society for the better. At the time, however, he had no idea how to put the practices he was learning about to use for the Mexican Americans and farm workers in America.

CHAPTER 3: GETTING INVOLVED IN ACTIVISM

Fred Ross and CSO

With a growing family, a good job, and respect from those in his community, it seemed as though Cesar Chavez had left his poverty-stricken farming days behind him. What he didn't know, however, was that a determined community organizer named Fred Ross was about to introduce Cesar to the world of activism and change.

Fred Ross was born in 1910 and founded the CSO (Community Service Organization) in 1948. He met Cesar Chavez in 1952, just four years after founding the organization. Fred wanted strong community organizers who would be able to fight for critical issues and rally poorer communities, showing them that they had power to change even against big corporations. A good organizer was capable of this,

Sí Se Puede

and more. Fred heard of Cesar in San Jose, California, and wanted to meet with him. He went by Cesar's house several times, but was always told by Helen that Cesar wasn't home.

Cesar, who was suspicious of the "gringo" who kept visiting his house, managed to avoid him for several days. Eventually, however, Cesar realized that Fred wasn't a "gringo" at all, and decided to attend one of Fred's weekly CSO meetings. At the meeting, he was majorly impressed by Fred's knowledge and belief that, through community organizing, the Mexican-Americans of California could change their status. Fred, too, was impressed by Cesar Chavez's intelligence, intensity, and passion for the subject. He knew almost immediately that Cesar was going to be an exceptional organizer, though he could not have guessed how influential Cesar would eventually become.

Cesar joined up and was soon devoting all his free time to CSO activities. One of their early campaigns was to register the Mexican-American communities to vote. Cesar went door to door, handing out forms and encouraging the members of his community to participate in the elections. This, however, was easier said than done. Many of the poorer community couldn't speak English, were not informed about candidates, or were intimidated by the process of voting. The republicans in the county were responsible for bullying potential voters, and harassing any who came to the voting polls.

In his first campaign, Cesar took control of the voter registration drive, registering over six thousand Mexican Americans in just three months. He openly protested the harassment being done to the poor and non-whites who were brave enough to show up at the voting booth. In retaliation, the Republicans accused Cesar of being a communist. This was during the McCarthy era, where paranoia was high, accusations were dangerous, and reputations could be ruined seemingly overnight.

It was a time of learning for Cesar, however, and he realized that just talking to people was going to get him nowhere. He came up with a new strategy to build power in the communities, and began a citizenship drive. He helped people with their problems, no matter how small or seemingly insignificant, and soon had a loyal following. When Cesar helped someone, he also empowered them, and encouraged them to make positive changes through example. In his early days as an organizer, this was the root of his power.

Sí Se Puede

Becoming an Organizer

Cesar became so involved in CSO, that he quit his job at the lumber mill and worked at the organization's office full time. He was officially a community organizer. In Oakland, he began hosting house meetings, and, although he was nervous, at his first meeting almost four hundred people showed up. He kept on, organizing a citizenship drive while continually being red-baited.

The rumors became so bad that even CSO began to pull away from him. Cesar stood firm, however, and even crashed a "trial" that CSO was holding to determine whether or not he was too dangerous to continue working with. When Cesar found out and showed up unannounced, he accused the leaders of CSO of being too scared to stand up for justice. Many of the middle-class leaders left after this, but the more determined ones stayed behind. After the accusations, Cesar decided that he would never hire a middle-class leader, because they were simply not as passionate about the issues as those who had experienced them first hand, as he had on the California farms.

Cesar began traveling, all the while keeping Madera as his home. He spent many weeks away from his family but grew tremendously as an organizer. Cesar became good at getting laws passed, and not just laws benefiting Mexican-Americans. Cesar had a passion to help people, and any time he saw a group or individual being discriminated against, he would do whatever he could to stop them.

In 1968, Cesar became involved in "project Oxnard", a campaign that lasted two years. This was his first significant undertaking against the grape growers who were hiring braceros (imported workers from Mexico) as cheap labor, leaving the locals without jobs. The government was involved in covering up the illegality of the practice, and it was easy for growers to take advantage of the situation.

Cesar knew that if he meant to break the illegal practices in Oxnard that he was going to need substantial proof in order to make any progress. He worked with many of the locals to gain extensive documentation and eventually decided to host a protest. It did not have any effect, though, and Cesar knew they needed something more. It was at this time that Cesar held his first march. The march was more powerful than strategies Cesar had tried in Oxnard previously, and would become an influential tactic for bigger battles later on in his activism career.

Sí Se Puede

Resigning from CSO

After nearly two years of working on Oxnard, Cesar had helped to file thousands of complaints against the growers. He wanted the CSO to help create a union for farmworkers, but they refused. Cesar left Oxnard and moved to Los Angeles, becoming the director there for CSO. When he came back to Oxnard only three short months later, all the progress he had made during that span of two years was gone, and the workers were in the exact same situation as before. It was then that Cesar knew for a certainty that the farmworkers of America needed a union, something that would allow more permanent change to be made not only in Oxnard, but throughout California and the entire United States.

Determined to make his union a reality, Cesar went to the AWA (Agricultural Workers Association) for help. A fellow organizer recruited by Fred Ross was involved with the AWA named Dolores Huerta. The AWA refused to help Cesar form a Union, however, and he turned once more to CSO for support. Cesar gave the CSO board an ultimatum that they organize the farm workers and form a union, or he would quit. CSO believed based on past experiences that forming a union was too high of a risk, and so, on his thirty-fifth birthday, Cesar made the difficult decision to resign.

CHAPTER 4: FORMING THE UNION

Gathering Strength

Cesar Chavez was not the first man to have the goal of forming a national union for farmworkers. In fact, there had been many attempts in the past, all unsuccessful. The collective agribusiness involved not just growers and farmers, but numerous industries from supermarkets to government organizations. This made agribusiness extremely hard to combat for poor farmworkers and laborers. In other industries, however, such as factory work, workers had the right to unionize under law. This same right did not exist for farm workers because of the immense influence of agribusiness in government and politics.

In attempting to form a union, Cesar Chavez was taking on what many, including CSO, deemed an impossible task. They took the previous one hundred and twenty years of failed strikes and attempts to form a union as proof that agribusiness could not be beaten. Cesar, however, used the previous failures as a learning opportunity. He attempted to get to the root of why the previous strikes had broken, and knew that he had to develop smarter strategies to take on the giant agribusiness and be successful.

Alone, with no income and no organization to back him up, Cesar moved his family to San Joaquin Valley in order to get started. His old community organizing teacher, Fred Ross, quit CSO and joined Cesar in San Joaquin. In the valley, Helen and the children worked in the fields and took care of the house, while Cesar held secret house meetings away from the growers. Often, Cesar would take Birdy, his youngest son, with him during the day. He knew that his decision to leave CSO was very hard on his family, especially Helen, but she supported him and his cause.

Slowly but surely, Cesar began to rally others to him. He recruited his cousin Manuel, convincing him to give up his job and join him. Both Fred and Manuel played big roles in forming the Union, and remained valuable allies throughout Cesar's journey. They distributed fliers, encouraged members of the community to write letters to the growers and politicians, and started the tradition of singing during union meetings. Cesar also became more involved in the religious community, and came to admire those who gave up all material possessions. From the very beginning, religion was extremely important to Cesar, and he knew that it would play a vital role in how successful his cause would be.

In September of 1962, after gaining enough support, Cesar Chavez called a meeting with many of his powerful friends. At the convention, they formed the NFWA, the National Farm Workers Association. They decided that their emblem would be a simplified version of the Mexican flag, with a black eagle against a red background. The eagle, present in more detail on the Mexican flag, was made up of absolutely straight lines for the union flag, and, therefore, was easier for everyone to draw. The color, red and black, signified strike in Mexico. There was controversy over the flag at first, as some thought it too closely resembled the communist flag, but the eagle stayed on and became the lasting symbol of the union.

The constitution for the union was adopted on January 20th, 1963, and the dues for the union were three dollars and fifty cents a month. With a name, an emblem, and twelve initial members, Cesar's union was born.

Sí Se Puede

The Grape Strike

Cesar Chavez's first strike was not actually in grapes, but against the rose industry in 1965. The strike broke quickly, however, but it was good experience for Cesar, who had never participated in or organized a strike before. On September 8 of 1965, the fledgling NFWA decided to support the Filipino workers who were going on strike from harvesting grapes. At the time, the NFWA had less than two hundred paying members, and it was uncertain whether or not their few funds could support a continued strike. Despite this, they supported it anyway.

On September 16, which was also Mexican Independence Day, the NFWA held a colossal meeting and agreed to go ahead with the strike. They began going around to labor camps, gathering support for their union, and also met with labor contractors and growers. The strikers formed picket lines and shouted for other workers in the field to join them. The growers, complaining that the pickets disrupted the productivity of the other workers, got the police involved. Arrests were made, and many of the strikers became nervous.

Even though some of the growers and cops threatened violence, or participated in minor harassment, Cesar taught his strikers not to be afraid, and never to respond with violence. Instead, they used the grower's violence against them, and publicized the unfair tactics that kept the union supporters from forming a peaceful picket. Others began getting involved in the strike, not just farmers. There were students who volunteered, and Cesar even managed to convince his brother Richard to join. Throughout the entire process, Cesar continued to emphasize the importance of non-violence and love.

The next month, in October of 1965, the grape boycotts started. Cesar knew that the strikers alone would not be successful against the powerful growers, even with media attention. To get the growers to take them seriously, they needed to get their attention by affecting their profits, which was exactly what the boycotts aimed to do. They sent organizers to many of the major cities, such as Los Angeles, Chicago and New York. To give the boycott a focus, the NFWA decided to boycott the biggest grape grower in Delano, a company called Schenley.

The boycott received national press, and the NFWA also received numerous donations to their cause. After the boycott had gone on for six months, it caught the attention of Senator Robert Kennedy, who personally got involved in several arrest cases in Delano, revealing the illegal tactics the police were using to arrest and convict picketers.

Despite the national attention and success of the boycott, the growers still weren't budging. Cesar knew that something drastic needed to be done in order to get their attention.

Three Hundred Miles to the First Contract

In order to draw even more national attention and support for their cause, Cesar embarked on a three hundred mile pilgrimage from Delano to Sacramento, the capital city of California. In Delano, many of the workers were afraid to go march with the group as there were police who tried to stop them in the middle of downtown. Once the press arrived, however, the police were forced to back off, and the march began. Cesar Chavez, along with seventy strikers, left Delano flying the Mexican, American, Pilipino flags, along with Union's black eagle and Lady Guadalupe, La Causa's patron saint.

That night they had their first meeting, where members were able to give speeches, and everyone sang and danced. These meetings would happen every night, and helped to keep the marchers motivated and excited. It was hard going, as marchers were forced to rely on the local townspeople for food and shelter. They were harassed by cars, and got blisters from walking in the heat. On the way, however, they talked to field workers as they passed, and recruited new supporters. Cesar actually got sick during the march, and, at one point, had to walk with a cane. He recovered on the fifteenth day, however, and continued the march all the way to Sacramento.

In the middle of the march, Cesar received a call saying that Schenley was ready to negotiate. Thinking it was a prank, they ignored it, until Schenley called again. Realizing they had a fantastic opportunity, Cesar and a few other leaders met Schenley in Beverly Hills to negotiate. Schenley agreed to recognize the union, and signed their first contract.

After twenty-five days of marching, and one significant contract later, they finally reached Sacramento. By the time they arrived at the capitol, over ten thousand supporters had joined the march and rallied on the steps of the capitol, drawing much national attention.

Merger

Although the union had made significant progress by signing Schenley, Cesar knew that it was only the first step. His goal was to sign all of the Delano growers, forcing them to recognize the NFWA as the farmworker's union. With their former target, Schenley, signed, the NFWA picked DiGiorgio as

Sí Se Puede

their next big target. DiGiorgio was a powerful grower with connections in the government and banking. He also had plenty of experience with breaking strikes, as he had broken several within the past twenty years.

The union turned their boycott on DiGiorgio, and began picketing his farms. Many workers were too afraid to quit working altogether, and so Cesar encouraged them to work as little as possible, thereby slowing down the harvest. DiGiorgio, used to strikers, was not afraid to get his hands dirty. There was violence in the fields, and DiGiorgio got the police involved in arresting picketers. It was during the DiGiorgio strike that a rival union controlled by the growers and agribusiness supporters in government, emerged. Known as the Teamsters, they spread discord among the farm workers and picketers alike, throwing the strike off balance.

When the picketers began talking about fighting the Teamster's violent harassment with violence of their own, Cesar was determined to stop it. He came up with the idea of holding daily prayer meetings, and encouraged as many as possible to come. The meetings were successful, and the talk of violence evaporated.

DiGiorgio, realizing that his harassment wasn't getting the job done, rigged the worker election to allow the Teamsters to win. The rate of arrests grew, and Cesar, after crashing a press conference held by DiGiorgio, was taken to prison for a short time. They began to fight for an equal chance in the election, even though DiGiorgio and the Teamsters were playing dirty. In the labor camps, workers were intimidated into choosing the Teamsters during the election. Many who refused were laid off and forced to go without work.

Cesar and his fellow leaders realized that, if they wanted to beat the Teamsters, they would need outside support. They attempted to merge the NFWA (National Farm Workers Association) with the AWOC (Agricultural Workers Organizing Committee). They had few problems finalizing the mergers, and Cesar Chavez became the head of the joined UFWOC (United Farm Workers Organizing Committee). With the merger, they had a much better chance of beating the Teamsters in the elections, although the odds were still against them.

When the Election Day arrived, the ballot showed the Teamsters, the UFWOC, or a No Union option. When the ballots were counted, the UFWOC won with over sixty percent of the votes.

Sí Se Puede

Influential Fast

The Teamsters were defeated for the time, and the UFWOC, having conquered DiGiorgio, were free to go after other growers in the Delano area. They went after Arvin Ranch, boycotted Derelli-Minetti and eventually decided to tackle Giumarra, the largest grape grower in California. The Teamsters were still present, constantly hindering the efforts of the new union, and their productivity entered a slump.

Giumarra refused to meet with the union to negotiate terms, and the union held a strike against him in 1967. They sent Dolores Huerta, a senior organizer, to New York in order to begin a boycott. When the boycott was successful, Giumarra decided to change the labels. Eventually, there were over a hundred labels, and it was impossible for organizers and consumers to track which grapes to boycott, and which grapes to buy. To solve the problem, the boycott shifted to all California grapes. The organizers in the cities began to picket large chain supermarkets, and the boycott began to take hold.

However, after two years of boycotting and picketing grapes with no significant results, whispers of violence began starting up again among the union. Cesar was so disturbed by the talk of violence that he stopped eating, and drank only water. He did not start out consciously intending to fast, but after a few days he knew that it was what he had to do in order to get the movement back under control. To Cesar, a fast was a very religious and significant decision, not only for religious reasons, but also cultural ones. In addition, Cesar greatly admired non-violent activists such as Gandhi, who were willing to put their own bodies on the line for their beliefs. To Cesar, nothing was more admirable. Once his mind was made up to stop eating, he did not know how long the fast would continue.

At first, only a few of his close friends knew that he was not eating; but, after four days of fasting, Cesar made an announcement at a union meeting. Everyone thought that Cesar was crazy, to attempt to halt the movement just when it seemed like they were about to have a breakthrough. Cesar, however, was firm. His dedication to non-violence was more important to him than the grape boycotts, and he retreated to a secluded cabin in order to rest until his fast was no longer necessary. At his cabin, he could lie down and still work. He held meetings and took visitors, all while lying in bed.

The news of Cesar Chavez's fast spread quickly throughout the union and the cause. To the Mexican Americans, who understood the cultural and religious significance of the fast, the news had an immediate effect. The talk of violence calmed down, and the rate of production significantly increased.

Sí Se Puede

Many Mexican Americans, but also politicians and other supporters across the country, began to fast with Cesar. The fast quickly brought the movement back to order, strengthened the boycott, and gave the people of the United States a new level of respect for the union leader, who was willing to follow in the footsteps of former spiritual leaders such as Gandhi so resolutely.

While the union and the grape boycott benefitted from Cesar's stand against non-violence, those closest to the suffering leader feared for his health. Many of his friends, and especially his wife, tried to get Cesar to stop the fast once there had been a positive effect on the community. A representative of the union even tried to force feed Cesar while he wasn't being watched. Cesar refused them all, however, and told them that he would stop when the time was right.

For the first week of the fast, Cesar experienced terrible nightmares and stomach pains. After about seven days, however, the pain and dreams were gone. He didn't even feel the need to eat, although he drank plenty of water. After two weeks, his joints began acting up, and he experienced terrible pain in his legs and arms. Yet still he continued to fast.

Despite the pain Cesar endured, he believed that suffering for others was the best way to help them.

His suffering was rewarded when a non-violent demonstration of prayer in court caused the judge to drop a case against some of the grape picket lines. He received letter of support from Senator Robert Kennedy, who was a strong supporter of their cause and a friend of Cesar's. When Cesar Chavez finally ended the fast on the twenty-fifth day, it was Robert Kennedy who appeared with him on national television. By the end of the fast, Cesar was too weak to stand, and had a written letter prepared for another to read because he didn't know if he was capable of speaking.

It was also then that Robert Kennedy decided to run for president, bringing hope to Cesar and his union that their cause would become a reality. Cesar's fast had been a wildly successful one; he had rallied the union to him, stopped all talk of violence, and gained national recognition. Many believe that, without the fast, the cause would have fallen apart and degenerated into violent squabbles and broken strikes like so many others had before.

CHAPTER 5: EXPANDING THE UFWOC

Political Tragedy and New Threats

After Cesar's twenty five day fast, he and the other members of the UFWOC were excited about Senator Robert Kennedy's decision to run for president. They believed that, with his election, they would finally be able to get the support they needed from the government to battle the growers and other members of agribusiness on equal ground. Their hopes, however, were dashed with Kennedy's assassination. The entire nation mourned his death, but especially Cesar and other supporters of the union. Richard Nixon was elected in place of Robert Kennedy, and, unlike the friendly senator, openly disapproved of the strikes and boycotts targeting California.

To make matters worse, Cesar's extended fast had left him in worse health than before. He was forced to spend months in bed due to severe back and spinal pain. The doctors couldn't figure out what was wrong, and so Cesar worked ceaselessly from his hospital bed. Eventually, a doctor figured out that one of his legs was longer than the other, and over the years had caused Cesar's spine to become misaligned from compensating for the difference. But until that point, Cesar remained bedridden. Meanwhile, along with Nixon's election, progress had declined in California. Growers were openly paying workers to oppose Cesar Chavez and his union, and got the government involved, as well. The UFWOC continued to fight in California, but by 1969, after four years of striking and boycotting grapes, morale was very low.

The union was targeting a significant grower named Steinberg, but since Cesar was bedridden, he was unable to attend the meetings. The negotiations fell through, and soon death threats against Cesar's life began coming in. Cesar, on some level, resigned himself to being assassinated, but they did everything they could to prevent such a tragedy from occurring.

Cesar still worked from his hospital bed, but was assigned guards twenty four hours a day. For additional protection, Cesar bought a German shepherd to guard him, as well. He trained the hound himself and named him Boycott. Cesar developed a close relationship with Boycott, who went everywhere with him. The next year he adopted another German shepherd, a female and named her Huelga. It was his relationship with the two dogs that would eventually lead to Cesar's decision to eat vegetarian, as well as to get involved in animal rights activism.

Conquering Delano

Even though morale was down among both the organizers and the farmworkers, they kept working in Delano. The union's efforts were being fought not just by Delano growers, but also the California State Board of Agriculture, which was doing a public campaign to oppose the union's boycott. While the organizers had many weapons at their disposal by this point, including striking, marches, and lawsuits, the boycott was their most effective weapon as it hit the growers where it hurt - their profit margins.

But by winter, even with the California government pushing against them, grapes were rotting on the vines because the growers couldn't sell them anywhere. Cesar and his organizers knew that they had the growers backed into a corner, and once again began negotiations. When Steinberg and several other major growers in Delano signed with the union, the grape growers began turning on one another. Grapes that had the union stamp on them in the grocery store sold as fast as supermarkets could stock them, but grapes without the stamp were still unable to sell.

Still not all of the Delano growers had signed with the union, however, and Cesar used his connections to schedule a large meeting. In mid-July negotiations started with over twenty companies, but the union's proposal was rejected. Meanwhile, the farm workers all over California were striking against more than just the grape harvest. Large strikes were done against both lettuce and lemon harvests, among others.

During the strikes and negotiations, the growers were not sitting idle. They brought in their own "union", which had significantly lower standards than Cesar's, and the UFWOC was forced into competition with the Teamsters once again. Cesar was afraid that the Teamsters would sign with all of California behind the union's back and that the farmworkers would be stuck with a false union controlled by the growers, a union that would keep them trapped in poverty and in terrible conditions. Eventually, despite the opposition, the UFWOC signed with nearly thirty Delano growers. The Teamsters, however, were not about to leave California.

Teamster Violence

In 1970, the Teamster union turned their attention to the lettuce fields, signing many growers. In response, Cesar and his union began protesting the grower controlled union using strikes, boycotts, and a march to Salina, California. To deal with the problem of the Teamster union taking over, Cesar had the headquarters of the movement moved to Salinas after the march and began to plan. They knew that a large strike would have to be implemented to have a chance, and also that they would have to make sure every farm in California had fair elections to nominate the union. These things, of course, were easier said than done.

Cesar, under pressure and being tricked by powerful growers, began yet another fast. Unlike his first successful fast, however, Cesar could not sustain his health and broke it off before the first week was up. He knew that if he continued to fast, he would die. With the need to recover his health, and Teamster signing contract after contract, things began to get serious for Cesar. Growers were firing workers who refused to support the Teamster union, and eventually it seemed as if a worker strike was imminent.

Knowing that the union could not sustain an extended strike, Cesar told his organizers to hold off the worker's strike as long as they could. He tried negotiating with the growers and called a large meeting, but they declared that they would not accept the UFWOC and insisted that the Teamster union was a legitimate union, and wanted by the majority of workers. Knowing full well that this was untrue, Cesar nevertheless tried to continue negotiations while holding off the strike.

During the summer of 1970, when the growers were still officially negotiating with Cesar and the UFWOC, the Teamsters began growing more aggressive. When several organizers attempted to contact farmworkers at a California broccoli farm, they were attacked by Teamster thugs and sent to the hospital. Along with this first significant incidence of violence, Cesar finally began to get angry. He stopped the negotiations since they were obviously going nowhere, and focused a boycott on the leading company named Chiquita.

After the talks degenerated, the Teamsters became even bolder. Their goons stopped picket lines wielding guns and chains to intimidate strikers, and a new leader appeared on the scene named Gonsalves. Head of the Teamster "goons", he drove around in a limo and spent money extravagantly. As violence began to break out all over the state, the other organizers began to worry about their safety, and especially the safety of their leader Cesar Chavez.

There were bomb threats, hospitalizations from those on the picket lines, and thousands of workers and unsigned growers alike threatened by the Teamsters. The chaos continued to build, and a Teamster organizer was shot. On November fourth, the UFWOC headquarters of Hollister was bombed. To the great disappointment of Cesar, the voice of anti-violence in the cause, serious violence had finally broken out.

Boycott, Jail Time, and Assassination Contracts

Backed into a corner because of the escalating violence, Cesar decided it was time to do something drastic to rally support and attention to what was going on in California. He purposefully began an illegal boycott with the intention of being sent to jail. He knew that there was a strong possibility of this outcome, and was warned not to eat the food in jail in case it was poisoned.

Sure enough, after finding out about the boycott Cesar was sentenced to solitary confinement in a small jail cell. Unable to work, he spent his time reading and adhering to a daily schedule. Because of his bad health, a doctor was sent for who provided him with a special diet to help him regain his strength. This way, Cesar also avoided being poisoned by the jail food. Even though he was in jail, he sent a message to the rest of the union to keep the boycott going and gain as much national attention as possible.

During his stay in the Salinas jail, Cesar Chavez was visited by many influential people, including the widow of Martin Luther King Jr., and Ethel Kennedy, Senator Robert Kennedy's widow. These visitors helped to bring valuable attention to the cause, and meanwhile Cesar waited for the courts to sort out the legality of the boycott and the injunction. Eventually, they decided the injunction was illegal, and Cesar was released from jail, to the great joy of his family and fellow organizers.

Due to the increased amount of attention on the boycotts and unions in California, the leader of the Teamster goons, Gonsalves, was investigated. The investigation resulted in uncovering a massive misuse of funds on the part of Gonsalves, as well as links between the Teamster organization, powerful growers, and the mafia.

Still, the government fought the UFWOC every chance they could using legislation, and after a time an assassination plot against Cesar Chavez was uncovered. The contract offered twenty five thousand dollars to a known assassin in exchange for Cesar's death. The public was not told about this information, and Cesar Chavez was hidden from the public eye. They moved him around from place to place as a precaution against the assassin named Buddy Gene Pronchnau.

The assassination contract was eventually confirmed and traced back to a man named Richard Pedigo, who was hired by the Delano growers to destroy the UFWOC. To do this, Pedigo hired an assassin to take care of Cesar Chavez and also planned on burning all of the Union records which would have seriously undermined the progress of La Causa. Pedigo was discovered by an undercover agent and arrested. The would-be assassin, Buddy Gene, was found, arrested and sentenced for life.

Leaving California

Despite all of California's attempts to shut down the UFWOC and stop Cesar Chavez by any means necessary, La Causa was so successful that it was able to expand to other farm areas of the United States. With expanding influence over the farming economy, however, even more powerful enemies against the union and Cesar Chavez were born.

Their unseen enemy was the American Farm Bureau Federation, a government body capable of coordinating legal blocks, and outlawing strikes, boycotts, and elections. Even though many of their weapons were limited or made illegal by the Agribusiness conspiracy, the UFWOC used all the methods available to them to fight unfair bills and government interference all across the nation. The UFWOC set up letter campaigns in Florida to fight anti labor bills, and revealed terrible work conditions on the other side of the coastal US. In Arizona, the motto "Si Se Puede" (Yes We Can) was born.

Back in California, the union achieved a significant victory when they successfully prevented proposition 22 from passing the California legislature. To make matters even better, President Richard Nixon, who had long opposed La Causa, resigned when the Watergate Scandal came to the public light. Nixon had often been seen with the Gonsalves, the head of the Teamsters, and had managed to do a lot of damage even without his full term as president. With Nixon, a powerful Teamster supporter, publicly disgraced, the movement, which had been in serious danger, once again had hope.

Sí Se Puede

Fighting the Teamsters

Even though the UFWOC had been successful in signing the majority of California growers, when their contracts were up in 1972, many of those same growers turned to the Teamsters, who were more powerful than ever. Many of the growers were signing with the Teamsters without holding elections, and later in the year even the Supreme Court acknowledged that the growers were using the Teamster union as a shield to prevent a real union from holding power.

Just as the UFWOC had won the first battle against the growers, Cesar and his organizers were determined to win this second battle against the false Teamster union. In 1973, the main battleground for the UFWOC versus Teamster battle took place in Coachella, California where the local government had made almost any action against the growers illegal. Cesar urged his supporters to purposefully break these unfair laws, and hundreds were arrested and jailed for their actions.

Soon the Teamsters began sending their goons to Coachella in mass, and eventually over three hundred and fifty Teamster thugs inhabited the city. They beat up helpless picketers while the police, who were with the local government and growers, sat by and watched. The level of Teamster violence escalated, and even the police forces stopped watching and got involved. They would provoke the lines by surround picketers and come at them with clubs, maces, and other weapons. The thousands who resisted were jailed, where they were treated horribly and unable to escape the beatings.

While violence was breaking out in the fields during the summer of 1973, Cesar was attempting to negotiate directly with the Teamsters in an effort to get them out of farming and out of California. The talks failed, however, when the Teamsters took advantage of the temporary truce and signed almost all of the Delano growers, who had previously been with Cesar's union, behind their back. Furious, Cesar and the union realized that the Teamsters had no intention of negotiating or even playing by the rules.

After the negotiation between the Teamsters and Cesar failed, the violence continued to worsen. Picketers were no longer being beaten but shot at. The Teamsters were targeting Cesar's family, and shot at his son who was out on one of the picket lines. With the violence growing worse, it was only a matter of time before tragedy struck. Two men died that summer; one was shot and another hit over the head. The death of these two victims, however, only served to make La Causa stronger and more focused than ever. They continued their boycotts, strikes, and pickets with renewed force.

Sí Se Puede

By September of 1973 Cesar was successful in coming to peace with the Teamsters, who agreed to leave California and the farming industry to the UFWOC.

Farm Workers Bill of Rights

After battling the growers, the government, and the Teamsters, the union was finally successful. They had organized both farm workers and American consumers, making them aware of the issues of La Causa. While their work would never be done, there were still many smaller battles to fight, the farm workers of America had a union that would ensure decent wages, living conditions, and working hours.

Cesar, after many long years of service, was rewarded for his efforts when he was called to visit the pope in Rome. Overjoyed, Cesar was granted a private audience along with several of his traveling companions, and the Pope thanked him for his services and his role in liberating the American farmer. Back in America, the Farm Worker's Bill of Rights was passed with support from both the growers and Cesar Chavez.

Animal Rights Activism

In the early 1970's, Cesar began raising two German Shepherds as guard dogs. His first, Boycott, became his closest companion during his later years. Boycott went everywhere with Cesar, who claimed to spend more time with the dog than with his own children. Cesar trained Boycott and Huelga himself, and his friendship with the two dogs opened his eyes to the world of animal rights by causing him to question how society treated animals. The two German Shepherds were more than just guard dogs trained as defense against the death threats and assassins, Boycott and Huelga were Cesar's closest friends.

After forming such a close relationship with his animals, Cesar could not imagine eating another sentient being and became a vegetarian. To Cesar, vegetarianism was a natural extension of the nonviolent beliefs that characterized all of his activism work. Cesar Chavez remained a vegetarian for over twenty five years, and some sources say that he was vegan for part of that time.

During his years as a vegetarian, Cesar spoke up for animal rights and converted many others to vegetarianism, as well. He shared his beliefs that animals should not be exploited by humans for any reason, including for food. Cesar realized that violence against animals came from the same place as violence against human beings, and believed that true peace would never be achieved by mankind so long as man misused animals.

In 1992, just one year before Cesar's death, he was awarded a lifetime achievement award in defense of animals. When he died the following year, he was buried in a grave next to his beloved German shepherd, Boycott. After Cesar's passing, many animal rights activists were upset that Cesar's strong beliefs on the treatment of animals and his overwhelming compassion towards them were overshadowed by his union activism. Many of his quotes about animal rights are still used by advocates of animal rights activism.

Family and Personal Life

Growing up, Cesar Chavez was surrounded by a large and welcoming family. The second son of Librado and Juana Chavez, Cesar was especially close to two of his siblings: his older sister Rita, and his younger brother Richard. These siblings helped support Cesar Chavez during his union years and got involved in activism, as well.

Cesar married his biggest supporter, Helen Fabela, in 1948. Helen was born and raised in Brawley, California, and was a first generation Mexican American. She worked in the fields as a young child, and so experienced first-hand the plight of the California farm workers. Cesar and Helen married after three years of inexpensive dates and seeing each other whenever they could. They traveled to San Jose and married in a church before going on a two week long honeymoon. After the wedding and the honeymoon, Cesar moved Helen to Delano where he had a steady job. They had a total of eight children, three boys and five girls.

When Cesar got the opportunity to work as a CSO organizer, Helen was the one who encouraged him to take it. She did this knowing that the family would live in poverty, and that she was going to have to be the main supporter and caretaker for their children. During her spare time, Helen made sure to stay involved with La Causa as much as she could, even if it only meant organizing papers or doing menial task work.

Because of the rigorous demands of his job, Cesar did not have much time to spend with Helen or their eight children. He spent much of his time traveling, organizing, or attending meetings. He knew that helping his people break out of the cycle of poverty was more important than being there for his family one hundred percent of the time, though he loved his family dearly. Even though it was extremely hard for Helen, she was always supportive of him.

Sí Se Puede

During his years working on the union, Cesar missed family dinners, birthday parties, and even left during one of his daughter's weddings to go to an emergency negotiation. Helen dealt with Cesar's absences, supported the family working ten hours a day on a farm, and set an example for many Mexican American women in the union. She was even arrested four times for her activism work. Even though Cesar would have been unable to accomplish his life's work without Helen's love, support, and dedication to La Causa, Helen receives little or no credit in the Chavez legacy.

Even though Cesar had been a semi-absentee father, after the children were grown many of them became involved in activism work, as well. Cesar worked with some of them when he was alive, his youngest son Anthony in particular, and after his death Helen, the children, and the rest of the Chavez family tried to hold the union together.

CHAPTER 6: CONTROVERSIES

Anti-Immigration Stance

Because the UFW was attempting to form a United States Farmworker's Union, Cesar Chavez and the union fought strongly against immigrants from Mexico. From the 1940's until the mid-1960's, the UFW fought against Braceros, native Mexicans who were brought across the border illegally by growers because they would work for much less than the American farm laborers. The efforts of the UFW to stop immigration at seemingly any cost continued into the late 1960's and early 1970's, when protests were held at the border, and UFW members formed lines to forcibly stop immigrants from entering the United States.

Because of the union's strong anti-immigration policy, many believe that Cesar Chavez was not the loving saint many people painted him to be after his death. Instead, they view Cesar Chavez as a hypocrite who was only interested in helping the California farm workers rather than truly fighting on the side of poverty and fairness for all. It is also suggested that Cesar, by limiting the scope of his union exclusively to the United States and farm laborers, proved that he did not truly understand capitalism and the globalization of the economy.

By not allowing the Braceros to work, Cesar Chavez and the UFW were condemning them to worse poverty in Mexico. By not allowing them to cross into the United States, they were keeping them trapped in the very same poverty they were fighting against in the United States. For these reasons, some do not agree with those who refer to Cesar Chavez with the same reverence as more well-known spiritual and religious leaders such as Jesus Christ and Gandhi and resent the fact that he is treated almost as a Saint in the State of California as well as in Latin American communities across America.

Disorganization and Paranoia

Although Cesar Chavez was undoubtedly effective at building the UFW during the 1950's and 1960's, a look into the later years of the union in the late

1970's and into the 1980's shows a lack of direction and an unraveling of the organization. While many do not acknowledge the rest of the story, well-acclaimed journalists such as Miriam Pawel provide documentation that the later years of Cesar Chavez's life gave way to paranoia, an extreme need for control, and disturbing religious cult activities.

In 1977, the first main break in the UFW occurred when Cesar Chavez openly supported Ferdinand Marcos, the president of the Philippines. Cesar visited Marcos, flying to Manila, and is quoted as admiring the man. This would not have been a big deal, except for the fact that Ferdinand Marcos was, in the view of human rights activists, a dictator controlling the country.

After Cesar's support of a possible dictatorship, many dedicated members left the union believing that Cesar was taking it in the wrong direction. The following year, more cracks became visible in the union as the organization lost many of their loyal followers. It wasn't until 1979, however, the Cesar began actively working against the organizers in UFW. The leaders in the union were organizing a lettuce strike in California, and Cesar, believing that it wasn't necessary, did everything in his power to stop them.

By the 1980's, it was clear that the union had completely lost its directive. Cesar Chavez had moved

Sí Se Puede

to remote La Paz and began showing signs of paranoia. He became obsessed with micromanaging the details of the organization, while at the same time hopping from one idealistic cause to another. He consistently was against the UFW having local chapters so that the farmers could govern themselves in their own areas.

At this point, his critics believe that Cesar couldn't accept that he wasn't needed in the union anymore, and was desperately trying to keep control and power in the organization as close to himself as possible. Many point to his quotes regarding suffering for others as proof that he believed himself above the common man by making himself into a martyr. There are hints that Cesar was fulfilled by his suffering, purposefully fasting and working long eighteen hours days because it was the only way he could be better than others.

While hiding away at La Paz, Cesar became close friends with Charles Dederich, the leader of Synanon, a drug rehabilitation program turned into a religious cult. Cesar admired the order and simplicity of Dederich's relatively isolated community, and began adopting similar cult tactics in the union. One of the most disturbing of these tactics Cesar adopted from Synanon was called "the game", an activity where a member of the cult (usually a former drug addict) was put into the middle of a circle. Once there, he was harshly criticized by the other members until he was completely broken down. This is a common type of strategy used by cults to make their members easier to control by their leader.

Cesar took his most trusted members to Synanon and had them participate in their own "game". Many put up with his antics, and those who didn't were considered traitors and "purged" from the community. In addition to taking the members to meetings in the cult, Cesar wanted all of the union members to live at La Paz, and with the help of a man named Chris Hartmire, tried to found his own religious order. His ideal situation consisted of those he deemed worthy living in a commune-like farm. He believed a "cultural revolution" was necessary in UFW.

In the end, the union became downright dysfunctional. The most able personnel were gone, and those who remained were subjected to Cesar's paranoia, anger, and delusions of religious grandeur. After Cesar's death, the UFW deteriorated into a power struggle between his many children. The union still exists in modern times, but no one would argue that it serves to benefit the farm workers, whose conditions have, for the most part, reverted back to the time before Cesar Chavez's leadership.

CHAPTER 7: DEATH AND LEGACY

Cesar Chavez died on April 23, 1993, at the age of sixty six. He was on a business trip in Arizona and died that night in his hotel room. Witnesses the next morning say it was a peaceful death, and that the book he was reading before he drifted off to sleep was still in his hands. Even though he died of natural causes, an autopsy was performed on his body to confirm that was the cause of death. The nation mourned Cesar Chavez's passing, and over ten thousand attended his funeral. Cesar was buried in Keene, California, and his grave can be visited at the National Chavez Center. Visitors can walk through the memorial gardens and visit the grave of the labor leader.

Cesar Chavez's humble lifestyle, non-violent beliefs, and dedication to La Causa made him an international icon for farm workers. The motto "Si Se Puede" is still inspirational to Latin Americans all over the United States. Streets, parks, buildings and schools are named after Cesar Chavez. Plays are performed in his honor, and in several states, including California, March 31 (Cesar's birthday) is officially recognized as a statewide holiday.

Cesar earned numerous awards and accolades during his lifetime, and the year after his death president Bill Clinton awarded the widowed Helen the Presidential Medal of Freedom in Cesar Chavez's place. Since his death in 1993, he has been honored by many influential men and women, including president Obama, who declared Cesar's birthday a national, rather than a state, holiday.

Even Cesar Chavez's critics recognize the importance of the man as a symbol, though the progress, which was won through his efforts in the 1960's, has largely diminished. In modern day, Cesar's children spend their time running businesses based on their father's legacy, and the UFW, although it still receives support, has only a few contracts. Without a strong leader to unite them through passion and faith, as Cesar Chavez once did, the union floundered. Despite this, Cesar's legacy remains, and his name is synonymous with hope.

CESAR CHAVEZ BIBLIOGRAPHY

Internet Sources

ufw.org

http://farmworkermovement.com/essays/essays/MillerArchive/032%20Profile%20Cesar%20Chavez.pdf

http://challengeoppression.com/2011/03/31/cesar-chavez-the-basis-for-peace-is-respecting-all-creatures/

http://www.pbs.org/itvs/fightfields/cesarchavez.html

http://www.theatlantic.com/magazine/archive/2011/07/the-madness-of-cesar-chavez/308557/

http://monthlyreview.org/2010/05/01/the-rise-and-fall-of-the-united-farm-workers

http://www.nytimes.com/learning/general/onthisday/bday/0331.html

Print Sources

Cesar Chavez: Autobiography of La Causa by Jaques E. Levy

Conquering Goliath: Cesar Chavez at the Beginning by Fredd Ross

The Union of Their Dreams: Power, Hope and Struggle in Cesar Chavez's Farm Workers Movement by Miriam Pawel

Documentaries

Fight in the Fields by PBS

CPSIA information can be obtained
at www.ICGtesting.com
Printed in the USA
LVOW12s1825251017
553729LV00004B/722/P